The Sky is Always in the Sky

By **KARLA KUSKIN**

Pictures by **ISABELLE DERVAUX**

A LAURA GERINGER BOOK
An Imprint of HarperCollinsPublishers

Previously published poems in *The Sky Is Always in the Sky* are from books
published by HarperCollins Publishers.

The Sky Is Always in the Sky
Text copyright © 1998 by Karla Kuskin
Illustrations copyright © 1998 by Isabelle Dervaux
Printed in the U.S.A. All rights reserved.

Library of Congress Cataloging-in-Publication Data
Kuskin, Karla.
   The sky is always in the sky / by Karla Kuskin ; pictures by Isabelle Dervaux.
      p.   cm.
   "A Laura Geringer book"
   Summary: Includes poems chosen by the author from previously published collections,
including "Soap Soup," "Near the Window Tree," and "Something Sleeping in the Hall."
   ISBN 0-06-027083-7. — ISBN 0-06-027084-5 (lib. bdg.)
   I. Children's poetry, American.   [I. American poetry.]   I. Dervaux, Isabelle, ill.
II. Title.
PS3561.U79S55   1998   95-45275
811'.54—dc20   CIP
                                                   AC

Designed by Christine Kettner
Hand lettering by Isabelle Dervaux
1 2 3 4 5 6 7 8 9 10
❖
First Edition
Come visit us on the World Wide Web:
http://www.harperchildrens.com

601603947

For Jool and Joel,
blue skies and love
—K.K.

To Lucien
—I.D.

CONTENTS

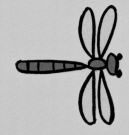

The sky is always in the sky,
the land is on the land.
The sea stays where
the sea should stay.
The world is nicely planned.
Brooks do not run in riverbeds.
The flower does not grow
into a spreading chestnut tree.
Corn doesn't peck the crow.
For if it did

or was

or were
it's obvious to see,
I might have been an elephant,
you might have been a me.
But I am me,
the tree's a tree,
likewise the plant's a plant.
And you are as you always were,
my dearest elephant.

"Cow" sounds heavy.
Cow
standing in the meadow
chewing.
A big fur box on legs
mooing.

Worm

is a term for worm.

It sounds like a worm looks

slow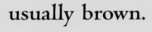

low to the ground

usually brown.

It would never have feathers

it would not sing at all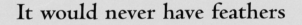

with a name like worm

it must be long and thin

and crawl.

I am beside myself
with glee.
I ho
and ho
and hee
and hee,
I hee
and hee
and ho
and ho.
I wonder why
I'm ho-ing so?

There is a me inside of me,

inside

the outside me

you see.

Thin or fat
fat or thin.
Open your mouth
and the food goes in.
And what you eat—
a bit of sweet,
a bite of stew—
each bite and bit
turns into you.

Put the dinner
on the table.
Then sit down and
eat it, Mabel.
And if you are able,
Mabel,
you may also eat
the table.

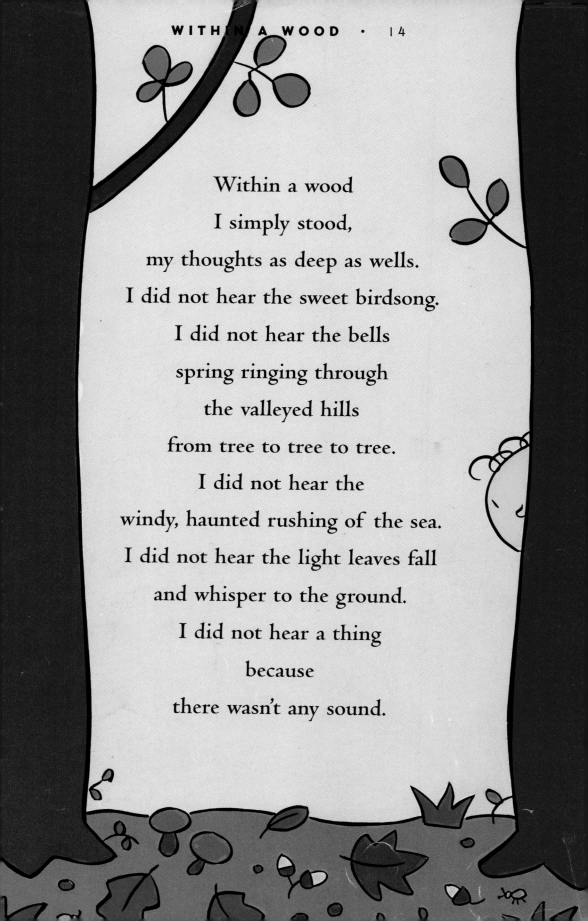

Within a wood
I simply stood,
my thoughts as deep as wells.
I did not hear the sweet birdsong.
I did not hear the bells
spring ringing through
the valleyed hills
from tree to tree to tree.
I did not hear the
windy, haunted rushing of the sea.
I did not hear the light leaves fall
and whisper to the ground.
I did not hear a thing
because
there wasn't any sound.

If I were a bird,
I would chirp like a bird
with a high little cry.
I would not say a word.
I would sit in my nest
with my head on my chest,

being a bird.

If I were a fish,
I would swim like a fish
silently finning
with nary a swish,
just finning through seaweed
to search for a free weed,
being a fish.

If I were a larkspur,

I'd stand in the sun,

growing up slowly

until I was done.

I'd rest in the breeze

with some leaves on my knees,

being a larkspur.

If I were a sandwich,

I'd sit on a plate

and think of my middle

until someone ate

me.

End of the sandwich.

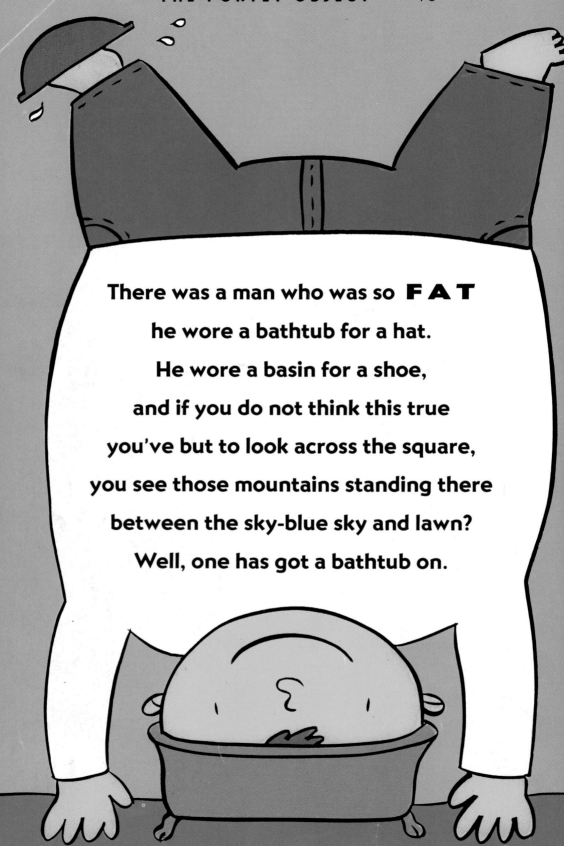

There was a man who was so **F A T**
he wore a bathtub for a hat.
He wore a basin for a shoe,
and if you do not think this true
you've but to look across the square,
you see those mountains standing there
between the sky-blue sky and lawn?
Well, one has got a bathtub on.

There was a hog

who ate a dog

and then he ate

a grass-green frog

and then he was so full

he cried.

And then he lay down—

bang—

and died.

A bear went walking
down the street
and everyone that bear did meet
that bear did greet
and also eat.

How sweet.

The dragon walks

for miles and miles.

He eats up people.

Then he smiles.

The dragon smiles

because he knows

that nothing tastes as good

as toes.

Counting the stars

as they glitter bright white

is lovely indeed

and a marvelous sight

when the air is as fresh

as the first night in fall.

But I always have a feeling

that comes very softly stealing

when my head with stars is reeling

that I didn't count them all.

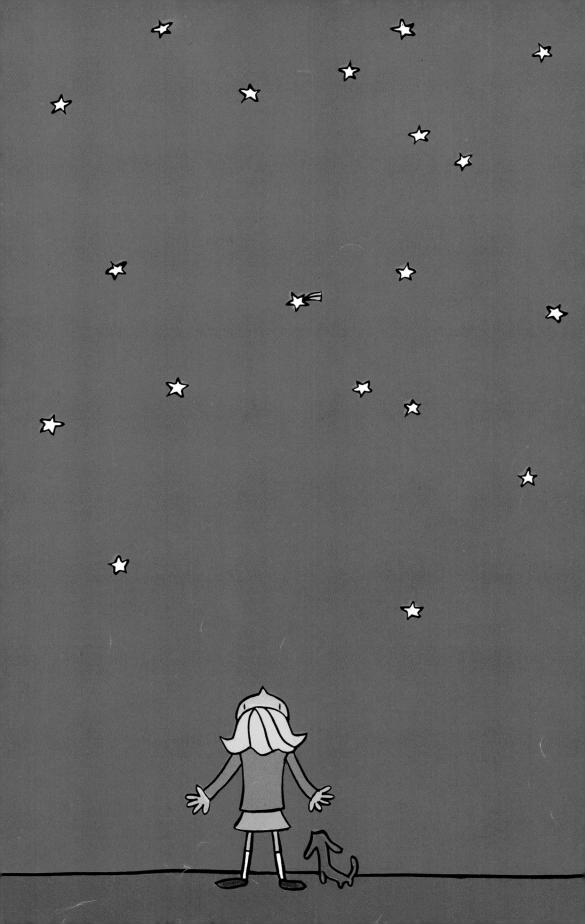

The streets are filled with mustached men

looking like each other.

Who?

The streets

are filled with mustached men

looking like each other.

Who?

The

streets

are filled with mustached men

looking like each other.

Who?

The streets are

filled

with mustached men

looking like each other.

Who?

Somebody gave me a hat.

It has three feathers and it's sort of flat.

I tried it on my brother.

I tried it on the cat.

And then I tried it on myself.

It looked too fat.

You may have it

if you'd like it.

It's a sort of fat flat hat.

Buggity
buggity
bug
wandering aimlessly
buggishly smug
when all of a sudden
along came a shoe
out with another shoe
wandering too.
The shoes went on
wandering:
left,
right,
left,
splat.

Bugs very frequently perish like that.

Spiders are all right, I guess,

or would be

if their legs were less.

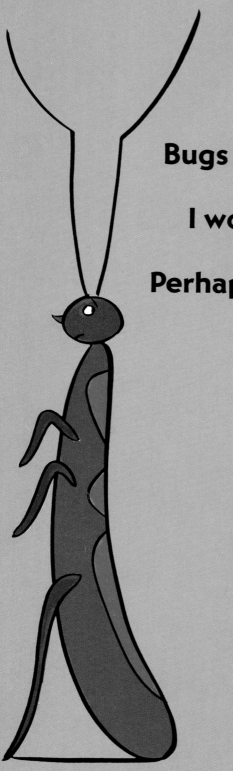

Bugs never speak.

I wonder why?

Perhaps they're shy.

A bug sat in a silver flower
thinking silver thoughts.
A bigger bug out for a walk
climbed up that silver flower stalk
and snapped the small bug down his jaws
without a pause
without a care
for all the bug's small silver thoughts.
It isn't right
it isn't fair
that big bug ate that little bug
because that little bug was there.

He also ate his underwear.

One jay

two jay

kitty got a blue jay.

Three jay

four jay

there isn't any more

jay.

Pigeons is a pretty word.

Pigeons.

Pigeons are a funny bird.

Pigeons.

Toeing out with silly care

shaped a little like a pear

inclined to cock small heads

and stare

at where?

Nowhere.

Pigeons.

Pigeons do not skim the sky.

It seems they'd rather hop than fly

though no one knows exactly why.

Pigeons.

Pigeons love a dusty crumb.

The fact is that

they're pretty dumb.

Pigeons.

Blue bird on a branch.

 Big bird on a twig.

Red bird on a ranch.

 Wild bird on a wig.

Broad bird on a bench.

 Bored bird on a pig.

Third bird in a bunch.

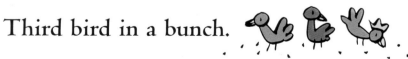 Blurred bird does a jig.

If you could be small

would you be a mouse

or a mouse's child

or a mouse's house

or a mouse's house's

front door key?

Who would you

which would you

what would you be?

Butter

butter

butter

butter

is a word

I love to utter.

I liked growing.

That was nice.

The leaves were soft.

The sun was hot.

I was warm and red and round

then someone dropped me

in a pot.

Being a strawberry isn't

all pleasing.

This morning they put me

in ice cream.

I'm freezing.

Write about a radish

too many people write about the moon.

The night is black

the stars are small and high

the clock unwinds its ever-ticking tune

hills gleam dimly

distant nighthawks cry.

A radish rises in the waiting sky.

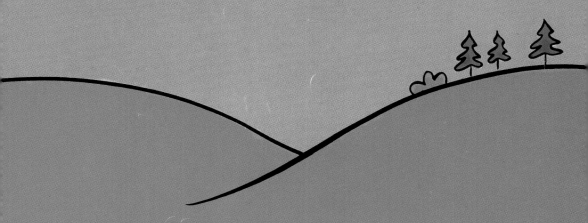

Under my hood I have a hat

and under that

my hair is flat.

Under my coat

my sweater's blue.

My sweater's red.

I'm wearing two.

My muffler muffles to my chin

and round my neck

and then tucks in.

My gloves were knitted

by my aunts.

I've mittens too

and pants

and pants

and boots

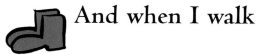 and shoes

with socks inside.

The boots are rubber, red and wide.

And when I walk

I must not fall

because I can't get up at all.

Catherine said,
"I think I'll bake
a most delicious chocolate cake."
She took some mud and mixed it up
while adding water from a cup
and then some weeds and nuts and bark
and special gravel from the park
a thistle and a dash of sand.
She beat out all the lumps by hand.
And on the top she wrote "To You"
the way she says the bakers do
and then she signed it "Fondly, C."
And gave the whole of it to me.
I thanked her but I wouldn't dream
of eating cake without ice cream.

The sound of a toad

in the road

in the mud

is a soft sort of thump

and a very wet thud.

Arthur sat in the mud all day,

his favorite way to sit and play,

and then when it was half-past four,

his mother, looking out the door,

said, "What is that that's sitting there?

Can it be a frowzy bear,

an old fur coat,

a mossy log,

quite lately risen from the bog?"

And Arthur with a little cry

burbled, "Mother, it is I,

Arthur Snap, your only boy."

And Arthur's mother wept for joy.

Rabbits

don't like rabbit stew.

I don't blame them much,

do you?

Many people who are smart
in physics, French and math and art
cannot tell two bugs apart.

Bugs are not very smart
in math or physics, French or art.
But *they* can tell two bugs apart.

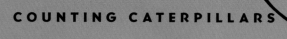

Counting caterpillars

as they climb the stalks of flowers

is easily accomplished

if you're free for many hours.

I am watering the plants.

I'm also watering the ants.

Wordless words.

A tuneless tune.

Blow out the sun.

Draw down the shade.

Turn off the dog.

Snap on the stars.

Unwrap the moon.

Wish leafy, sleeping trees good night

and listen

to the day shut tight.